Back When
for
Now

Marissa Madrid

iUniverse, Inc.
New York Bloomington

Back When for Now

Copyright © 2010 by Marissa Madrid

iUniverse books may be ordered through booksellers or by contacting:

iUniverse
1663 Liberty Drive
Bloomington, IN 47403
www.iuniverse.com
1-800-Authors (1-800-288-4677)

Because of the dynamic nature of the Internet, any Web addresses or links contained in this book may have changed since publication and may no longer be valid. The views expressed in this work are solely those of the author and do not necessarily reflect the views of the publisher, and the publisher hereby disclaims any responsibility for them.

ISBN: 978-1-4502-1818-4 (pbk)
ISBN: 978-1-4502-1817-7 (ebk)
ISBN: 978-1-4502-1816-0 (hbk)

Printed in the United States of America
iUniverse rev. date: 3/29/10

Dedicated to the loving memory of my grandfather, Pete Madrid, who taught me to laugh, love, and live with no fear, and to my son, Nathaniel (Nate the Great), who shares Gramps's same birthday and inspires me to be my best.

Introduction

I have worked with children of all ages for eighteen years, and there has never been a dull moment in my field as a teacher, advocate, and community liaison. It has been one rewarding ride. I have always made it a habit to keep my childhood close to heart for a better understanding of those I take care of. I ask myself, "How would I have coped with that situation?" or "I remember how happy it made me when someone did that for me." No matter what we choose to dwell on, one simple fact remains. As children, we all had beautiful, creative, hopeful, and imaginative minds. We still have the ability to regain our grasp on that optimism, attitude, and posture to claim "everything is possible."

I too have met my challenges, starting as long ago as I can recall life; all the way back to two years old. One of the greatest aspects of my life is that my Grandparents adopted and raised me. This had a dual impact on my journey through all ages, considering the generation gap between the elderly couple and me had provided quite a few conflicts of interest. And, on the other side, I would not give up one of part of being raised by them; with gratititude for having the opportunity to pass on the same nurturing, values and traditions to Nate.

At one point, I remember my family members and some friends in hostile states of transgression, and I knew in my heart that this was not what I wanted. I made an agreement with myself about what I didn't want to feel and what I refused to become. I have no idea what gave me the ability to think this way at such a young age, but it came to pass when I made the choice to live in the solutions and not the problems. Now my daily efforts consist of my personal motto of *inspiring and empowering others to achieve*. This can be a tall order, depending on who I am working with: my son Nate, colleagues, and parents. I like to perceive what I do as a giant life puzzle, where I connect individuals, programs, and resources for the greater good of everyone I know and meet. It occurred to me that creating *Back When for Now* could be another light-hearted extension of my mission to reach others. I do not enjoy rehashing stories of *why* there is a lack of anything. Instead, let us consider and recognize some of the turning points when we lost faith, belief, and hope in our dreams and visions. In place of focusing on why we *can't* do what we love, focus on how and why we *can*.

As you advance through the pages, you will discover each section is divided into three parts as follows:

- Reflections: Personal stories intended to take you into the past for inspiration and potential lessons you may have overlooked.

- Journal: Brief thoughts and ideas to redirect you toward positive thinking, cognitive learning, and sometimes moments of secret giggling.

- Hands on Senses: Activities to explore, experiment, and create as you use your senses to navigate away from lost awareness of youthful fun. In this part, you are invited to rekindle your childlike perception of the world through all of your senses … including common sense.

I have left this layout open ended for you to use at your leisure and so you can approach the activities with ample time to truly enjoy the results. Keep in mind that most of the Hands on Senses are derived from simple children's activities. So, forget about looking immature or anything of the sort. This is intended for you to cut loose, have fun, and be as childish as you want.

As you peruse the pages, please also note that there is an undertone for parents, educators, leadership program participants, and others as a vessel to reconnect with the youth in the community. *Back When for Now* is an all-age-appropriate tool for multipurpose use. Bring out the kid in you and uncover how you came to this second, where you can create you life's masterpiece: *you.*

Marissa in Valdez, CO 1973

My Path

A child carries on through life, accepting contentment and tragedy alike. She ignores harsh criticism and discouragement for loving the world and readily forgiving others. She perceives life as a universe to explore and to merge with. Often misunderstood, she is called a dreamer, confused, scattered, and aloof. She is not blind to the opinions and actually finds a sense of pride in the titles. To her, they define freedom and proof of her tenacity to continue gripping it tightly. She evolves into a young lady and encounters a new stage in which she chooses not to protect herself, although she encourages the dreams, goals, and achievements of others. Though her heart is mutilated by even those closest to her, she holds onto the dreamer and smiles in every end. She knows she is remembered as loving and compassionate. Some years pass, and the grown woman still possesses the uncanny ability to push others into feats of great heights and measure. She believes that even without immediate results, they too may grasp the message and pay it forward. What others see as a curse or bad luck, she embraces to demonstrate zeal and desire for passion in every act. Again, she transforms into a mother. Such bliss she experiences to observe the milestones and memories of the child, who will someday become a good man. He too faces the same ridicule of being different … sensitive, courageous, and an old soul. She diminishes his doubts, and he walks with bold posture and confidence. Her work is good. Now she only occasionally struggles with balance. She is too many minds in one for most people to know. Every day is simply another phase in her poetic life of private and introverted leaps of faith. She is that one most can't help but to wonder about, even briefly. She is deliberate and strong in advocating for what is just, and humble enough to admit when her best couldn't prevail. She is an artist of many media, creator of what most consider tedious (or never notice), photographer, writer, painter, and knotter of satin cords. She is a lover of nature, embracing its existence on a spiritual basis and connecting to the intertwining of scents and breezes. She is music to the core of a struck chord and melody rupturing deepest emotions of all spectrums, and into the air as the fondest of memories. She is maybe a flower or, perhaps, a thorn even once removed, leaving a faint scar or sign of a moment in laughter, adrenaline, or slight silence to ponder.

Here's Looking at You:

In this section about the visual sense, you will be presented with the most important intention of this book, which is how you perceive, believe in, and promote your strengths in everyday life. Visual and symbolic media often help individuals make a stronger connection to cognitively retain more concepts, theories, and ideas. For this exact reason, you are provided with easy and meaningful activities, which are more than memories of something witty heard or a one-time inspiration. Since infancy, colorful and unique objects hold our attention. As we continue to grow into a child who strives to make independent decisions, we also choose items of bright, vivid, and flamboyant colors. Even advertisers have historically utilized this approach, with the bright red bike and the pony covered in a rainbow of flowers enticing children with must-have items.

Everywhere you look, there are characters on cereal boxes, hair accessories, and gripping commercials targeted at the child's eye. We are naturally drawn to visual stimulation, which leads to imagining pictures, extending the experience of the mind.

Using the media, you are invited to access your memory of the positive events that not only escorted you to who you are now, but also to open the doors you may have closed due to social conformity, fear, or doubt. Open your mind to the childlike ideas of creating something that is your visual, spiritual reminder of how good it felt to see the world with fresh eyes then, of how fortunate you are now, and to embrace the changes you can make for greater tomorrows. Have fun!

Reflections:

When I met theatrical performer and violinist Jesse Wilson, we discovered that we were both interested in the arts and were committed to the community. Soon, we launched his monologue production of "Jesse Stories." Merging my educational experience and his talent to deliver meaningful stories, we began to partner with educators and professionals to enhance educational and life concepts within their organizations. In just twenty-four days, he performed for five types of audiences and momentum took flight.

One morning, Jesse called me and we discussed the fact that we were approaching some bigger names and reputable organizations. Our initial thought was that we should seek out endorsements from two of our partners in the field. Then we rethought that concept after I told Jesse, "All that we have accomplished to this point has been through our own merit and without any endorsements. You know the cliché 'significant other'? Well, Jesse, I strongly believe in your work, and you do not need to lean on the name of others to be significant. Working with faith in our mission is producing the sought-out results. Let those organizations see that we have made a great impact on the community by independently promoting Jesse Stories, and they will readily invite us to partner with them. Besides, what if they didn't exist? Then who would we rely on to put *your* name on the map?" After this brief exchange, we went right back to work, and Jesse has been very successful in his theatrical campaign. Through his inspirational performances, many individuals are being exposed to momentous stories in the art of theatre and, more important, about the art of life. He truly has mastered challenging his audience's thoughts in an effort to bridge the gap between all ages and stages, in addition to the stage production of *Face the City*. In this performance, Jesse provides a monologue of a journey in life with a painterly effect to the mind's eye (listed in the resource section toward the end of the book.)

Jesse Wilson perfoms for a group of preschoolers with his violin and story telling at West Community Center.

Journal:

Many people focus on what they want and what they don't possess, with little or no gratitude for what they already have. Others feel that they are required to only request or beg for miracles from a higher power, a number of times a day, and their wish will be fulfilled with no work involved. Here are a few quotes about the reoccurring message to have faith in all that you do and to be rewarded for the love placed in your work:

- "Success depends on your backbone, not your wishbone" (Unknown).

- "Every man's work shall be made manifest" (1 Corinthians 3:13).

- "Your work is to discover your work and then with all your heart to give yourself to it" (Buddha).

- "Your profession is not what brings home your paycheck. Your profession is what you were put on earth to do. With such passion and such intensity that it becomes spiritual in calling" (Vincent Van Gogh).

The gray area society has imposed is that you cannot succeed without the acceptance or the approval of others. Some of you may think that you do not have a vision outside of getting a promotion or raise, or simply making it to your next break. But if you are honest with yourself, you can think of three great ideas that you had in the last few years. You probably just dismissed them as passing thoughts. A common theme among most individuals is, again, taking the advice from others who say your vision won't work because their friend's mother's brother's son's grandma tried it and failed. We are all so fortunate that great leaders in our history chose to do the *impossible*, in spite of what the majority assumed (assumptions based on fear). Cheers to the artists, inventors, mentors, and leaders who have brought us to a place of opportunity as far as our minds can reach. No matter how impossible you think your ideas are, write down the top three.

Then, narrow down your three ideas according to what most intrigues you, or what stirs your passions into a completely imaginary canvas. Do not wait for someone else to give you permission to make something happen, or to succeed. Write or map out the *big picture* vision. Describe the final result or product with infinite details of what you see, hear, and feel. When you work from the end, all the pieces fall in place with your faith in not only the project, but more so in your abilities to start it. You can modify and rearrange everything as you go. Remember to be grateful for what you have and to believe in what you will gain.

> *God gave man an imagination to compensate*
> *him for what he is not; and a sense of*
> *humor to console him for what he is.*
>
> **—Anonymous**

Hands on Senses:

Now, on the more entertaining side, let's time warp to *back when*. Who was your favorite action hero? I thought Wonder Woman was pretty cool in her invisible jet. For some reason, though, my invisible jet could never fly over anyone I tried to evade (no matter how hard I pushed on the imaginary remote control in my hand).

So, what if you did have superhuman powers and you could be a hero? What would your name be? What would your costume look like? What would you change or create more of? Guess what? Hero and Heroine, you exist! You were on your way to impacting the world around the ripe old age of five. Gravity (challenges) couldn't resist your flight (success), and all the antagonists (doubt) fell to the ground in defeat. You could make things of all colors and discover natural phenomena in your adventures. Grown-ups were too serious, and older kids were scared to pretend for the sake of their reputation (being called a "baby" has that effect). Time stood still for you, and the world was yours. Try the following:

1. Take out your box of markers, crayons, or colored pencils and a blank sheet of paper.

2. Draw an image of you as a hero performing a major mission (don't worry about your drawing skills).

3. Write your hero name in big letters at the top and remember all the details surrounding you: people, buildings, word bubbles (make it your living comic strip).

4. Be your own best critic and dare to frame your hero masterpiece.

5. Hang it!

Marissa as heroine *Mega Mama*,
drawn in her characature.

I know you're thinking that you wouldn't even remotely consider hanging it, and you may be worried about explaining what it is to others who ask. This is actually the fun part. I tried this out on my family, and the results were rewarding. When Nate saw it hanging in my office, he took time to read the word bubbles and really studied the details. That same evening, he pulled out all of his art materials and created his own picture. He was a bit more creative in using a combination of drawings with crayons and markers and magazine cutouts. His laughter and the stories that surfaced were priceless.

Now, my no-nonsense friend, on the other hand, looked at my master's canvas with an expression of "What the heck?" He's not exactly artistically inclined and possessed a "black-and-white" demeanor, as he put it. Yet, every time he looked at it, he grinned and shook his head. I can take this one of two ways. Either he admired my desire to create with no regard to opinions, or he thought I was flat-out silly. What matters is that I am fine with both possibilities because it's fun being me, and in the end, my goal was to stir up some humor …with an undoubtedly priceless and historical image landing in a museum some day.

Nurture your mind with great thoughts; to believe in the heroic makes heroes.

—Benjamin Disraeli

Hammering Thoughts

Reflections:

The world you perceived as a child remains yours. I'm not indicating that you can dismiss responsibilities or deadlines. You can, however, regain the same strong convictions of your goals and your ability to create, and independently pursue what you know, deep down, is intended for you.

Envision one thing given to you in your youth that made you feel loved, nurtured, and perhaps even invincible. In the following story, note that gifts also come in the form of encouragement, wisdom, and mementos that you carry in your heart, and they have become part of who you are today.

I recall watching my grandfather repairing an old piece of furniture when I was around seven. I experienced such calmness in his presence as he included me in his tasks. The scent of wood as he sanded, the precision of hammering small nails, and the vision of his hands working the wood to somewhat of a sculpture are all with me as I reminisce about the special moment. He always shared stories as he worked; one day, he said, "I took a walk the other day and I saw one of your friends playing in her yard. She had some type of red plastic toy and destructively tossed it, till within seconds it broke. I think that maybe she has been given too many things that she doesn't need. Not all gifts can be held in your hand … and if they can, the gift should come with a meaning. There is always a right tool for every job. Take a large piece of wood; it requires larger tools to size down the pieces needed to make the chair. I cannot use a big hammer to nail these small nails for fear of damaging the decoration on the chair's leg. The small hammer is my choice for the job so I do not cause damage, which is why it's called a finishing hammer. Sometimes, people think you finish everything with a big bang. I think one should tend to the final details with a gentle touch to avoid destroying the entire piece." He then placed the hammer in my hand and said, "You can have it."

It was like accepting an ancient scepter ruled by his hand for many years. I have always kept it handy (including in my Jeep), and it has always been the perfect tool in the least expected situation ... even as I hold it to feel closer to my royal hero, Gramps.

Gramps's Hammer

We don't receive wisdom; we must discover it for ourselves
after a journey that no one can take for us or spare us.

—*Marcel Proust*

Journal:

With that precious memory of what was given to you, write in your journal the events that led to and followed the happy moment. Was it something you requested or secretly wished for? Were you amazed, surprised, or maybe a little shocked that the moment came to pass? When you received it, did you protect it or linger in it for days, weeks, or months? Do you still have it (whether actually in your hand or just in your mind)? The point is that your ideas and curiosity about creating something of your own are gifts. They should be nurtured, protected, and acted upon the second you accept them. Creating is our trademark as humans, and when we share our creations, the gift of inspiration multiplies within others.

Hands on Senses:

Go to a local hobby store and find beads that *call* to you. The wonderful thing about beads is that they know no gender and are so diverse in purpose. As small as they can be, they offer a great sense of happiness. Experiment with various threads, or chains, or whatever intrigues you. Your local library carries some great books if you are looking to do more than just string beads. Create your own little memento that you can have handy at all times (necklace, bracelet, keychain, bookmark, etc). This is also a fun way to express your appreciation for others, and it is very rewarding when you see them wearing or using the piece you created.

Whatever you choose to make should be a reflection of your personality. Think of it as a symbolic measure of your commitment to start implementing your ideas. It is the same concept of starting with a center bead, and the others follow as you create something functional and meaningful.

Make what works for you. Here are but a few
pieces I made with an assortment of colors and
designs used in wire wraps, knots, and threading.

Candid You

Reflections:

Would you wake up at 5:00 AM to watch the sunrise until the warmth is felt on your nose or park somewhere to watch the changing colors of a sunset until the first twilight star? My answer to both questions is yes. My colleagues and friends think I'm nuts to indulge in watching the sun rise and think I have too much time on my hands if I watch the sun set. Time is on our side when we choose to embrace doing what we love. Do you make time for TV, video games, and other things? It is not bad to watch a wonderful movie or an occasional episode of a how-to program. But why stifle your personal progress and take away from the opportunity to grow and live in your own drama, mystery, or action? The commonsense answer to this question is that most people want to escape their current phase of life, instead of actively changing it. Most will sit and wish for vacations, dream homes, a new car, winning the lotto, and so on. Change requires action and believing in the outcome that you do not yet see.

They always say time changes things, but you actually have to change them yourself.
—Andy Warhol

Collage of photos all taken at Emerald Lake, CO

Choose up to 7 photos you captured on a nature walk/hike and lay them out on a poster board.

Paste them down followed buy cut out words written/printed on colored paper (peace, abundance, fresh air, abundance, or what ever comes to mind when you look at the photos). For a more tactile affect, ad a few of the nature samples you collected. Get creative as you'd like and it can be your openly displayed nature collage.

Journal:

Once you have completed the collage, look at it from a distance and notice all of nature's elements that go through change. Document these changes in your journal; describe the similarities and differences in contrast to adjustments you make. The intent behind this activity is to reconnect with your natural and instinctive environment, seeking clarity of thought and inner peace of spirit, and embracing the basics that lead to everyday necessity. Write three realistic changes you will begin tomorrow morning.

Hands on Senses:

Going back to the sunrise and sunset, what details would you observe? Dive into nature with a camera (you can also collect a few nature pieces like leaves, pebbles, and twigs) and rediscover all the things you recognized as a child. Seasons turning, caterpillars changing into butterflies, snow melting, pine needles falling from trees: they all change for the greater good of their surroundings. As you open up your senses, note that you are actively a part of everything you see in abundance. Would this abundance exist without being necessary to our survival (accumulation of infinite drops of water feeding the foliage to provide all living things with oxygen, and so on)? No amount of paper we push will ever equal the abundance of earth's life … though we could refocus and contribute to her cause of trying to support ours.

Your thoughts, senses, and actions play a role in a vast open space where you too are imposing changes you may not even see. This is a natural phenomenon, which takes place whether you want it to or not. Compare this concept to how your body responds to cold weather by shivering, the sweat on your brow when you eat spicy foods, or sneezing caused by excessive scents. In every second, we are actively connected and interacting with everything in our environment, as we all breathe the same air. So, walk with awareness and a purpose to make productive, positive, and continuous results. Stand by the importance of your goals and embrace your walk as a grand production in the art of life. What will your next change be?

Choose up to seven photos you captured on a nature walk and lay them out on a poster board. Paste them down next to cut-out words written or printed on colored paper ("peace," "abundance," "fresh air," "abundance," or whatever comes to mind when you look at the photos). For a more tactile affect, add a few of the nature samples you collected. Get as creative as you'd like, and openly display your nature collage.

You must welcome change as the
rule but not as your ruler.
—Denis Waitley

Actions, Not Titles

Reflections:

When I chose to start a home business as a Community Liaison and Artist, my family and friends made subtle suggestions that my chances of success were next to none. What they didn't know was that I was very ill and had hidden it the majority of the time. I needed to find something that suited my need for healing time and provided an income that would match my efforts. As a teacher, I was very dedicated to my students and felt a sense of duty to find every possible means to extend their development. This included spending some nights without sleep, having an inconsistent eating schedule, and accommodating families after hours.

I observed these discouraging people very closely. Clearer than their words was their display of body language. This is what told me that they were genuinely concerned, but they all based their opinions on assumptions, rumors, and fear of failure. I responded to them with a question I once heard, "Would you ask a poor person for financial advice?" That question is not meant to insult those who suffer economic struggles. It's the principle of having the common sense to follow the advice of the proven, instead of hearsay.

Now, here I am, still helping families and communities as a volunteer since I followed my calling (at this point, I hope you recognize my theme of not worrying about acceptance, permission, or approval from others). The best part is I haven't been ill in quite some time, and I have the luxury of being consistently present for my family (I always hated when my supervisor asked me if someone else could tend to Nate when he wasn't well, just to accommodate a staffing or scheduling problem).

Journal:

As a child, what did you *think* you wanted to be as an adult? Was it to be a great leader, a humanitarian, or maybe just rich? This question has nothing to do with titles, but with actions. Titles are a good way to understand someone's primary responsibilities, but they do not describe all of the tasks that person undertakes. In other words, travel back to when you imagined not only your role as an adult, but how you acted it out. See a time when it was all your way and you made all the rules to become this all-knowing, brave, strong, and helpful grown-up (this can include the moments you daydreamed). Describe that part of you that was projected during your dramatic play and all of the empowering emotions you experienced. What did you create, invent, discover, or build?

The beauty of this phase in childhood is that once we transform into our ideal grown-up, we see every task as a part of us: ambition, passion, and endless possibility. The tasks aren't seen as a burden of responsibilities or social pressures, but as actions we proudly stand by. No adult can convincingly tell you that it is impossible to become rich, that it is not secure graduating with anything less than a master's degree, or that you are only successful if you become what they want (I still cringe when I hear those claims by today's parents).

How close are you now to being what you envisioned? Again, I am not talking titles here. Do you help, empower, create, or do any of the things you envisioned as a child? List those things that you have embraced and set into motion as a way of everyday life. As an example, when I was a little girl, I wanted to perform the duties of a medical professional: take care of others, be kind, and help others feel better. Once in my teens, I discovered that I could do these same things as a teacher (as I learned in my first childcare job), with more possibilities suiting my personal skills. This made even more sense to me because what I provided to the children could be multiplied as they shared what they learned with others as an ongoing process for years to come.

Love what you do, and no job description is worthy of your actual efforts. Actions define the person perceived, not titles.

> **Respect yourself and others will respect you.**
> **—Confucius**

Hands on Senses:

Do you wish you could have a job that you actually feel great about? At one time or another, we all do. Though most of us cannot just up and leave, you can improve your current perception of "days in paradise."

1. Write ten things you like about your position, work environment, colleagues, or whatever comes to mind (a challenge at first for some, but be fair to the good things). These are the things you would like to have in your next workplace as well.

2. Write ten other things you would like to have in your next work adventure: more money, more time, friendlier staff, a more efficient team. Add those details to the first ten.

3. Now, if you could place all these desired elements in a treasure box, what would they look like? What would symbolize each detail? Lost? Here are some examples:

- More wealth = gold coins, Matchbox car, or picture of dream home

- More time = clock, mini hourglass, or calendar

- Fewer walls and more view = magazine cutout of mountains

- Shorter driving distance = piece of a map

These are all items you can find (remember the little action figures or dolls and their accessories you enjoyed as a child?) at the hobby store, at a thrift store, or maybe even in a box you put in back of the closet. Once you have collected all the small-scale items representing what you already like or want more of at work, display them in one of the following ways:

- Put them in a shadow box you can hang: This one is perfect since it can be seen easily and remind you daily of what you are already grateful for and what you have to look forward to.

- Turn a shoebox into a treasure chest, containing your "work mementos": This is more interactive since you will have to physically (and consistently) open the box and actually take the items out to reflect upon them.

So now you may think, "How in the heck will this change my attitude toward wanting something better?" Well, as challenging as it can be, there is always something positive to find in every situation. The concept is to be grateful for what you already have. Not to mention, it makes your list of wants seem less lengthy and easier to approach since you have already acquired half of them.

Now start considering how to approach *getting* those other things, and look at your options. Is there another field that interests you? Do you have the option to start a home business? Do not doubt yourself; believe that everything is possible (just like you did as a kid). You will never know what could have been until you take that leap out of fear. Do not fear the possibilities; only fear your lack of will to explore them.

You will find that you have the power to make things happen. Step out of your comfort zone and try something new and creative. Coworkers can be like family, in the way that we can't always choose them. Every individual has at least one good quality that you appreciate. Expressing your gratitude for those qualities can make things happen (at least more harmoniously).

1. Pick up a decorative notepad or a pack of thank-you cards.

2. Write down the names of your coworkers and one thing they do that is inspiring, helpful, or admirable (always smiles, volunteers, remains positive, etc.).

3. Write a note in the card or on the decorative notepaper to each person, thanking or praising them for their effort or for what they do to make things better.

4. Distribute them in person or discreetly in their mailbox (the second choice adds more to the surprise). You do not need a holiday as an excuse to give small tokens; remember how it felt to receive a card, letter, or note when you were growing up? Small acts of kindness reward *both* the receiver and the giver!

This is but one example of how you can express gratitude. Some people may react by doing more, being more approachable, or acting more receptive. Don't feel bad if others do not react at all … it's nothing personal. Oh yeah … just like when we were kids, leave the boss (or the teacher) last if you want to thank him or her, to avoid being seen as the "teacher's pet."

Leadership and learning are indispensable to each other.
—John F. Kennedy

A Child's Message: Once Upon a Voice

Another way we learn is through listening. Not just hearing, but actually listening. Okay, I that know this sounds like a game of "state the obvious." But seriously, think for a moment how we fine-tune our ability to process and learn from sounds. A variety of words are used to communicate precise information. A baby crying lets us know she or he needs to be changed or fed. We listen to sirens, phones, and "you got mail" to alert us, and so much more! Wow, how do we handle so much information that is transmitted to our brain every second of the day?

So here's an opportunity to refine our skills, not what we accept as the daily norm, but what we've lost over time by using the mental autopilot trigger. This chapter explores how we can retain more information, develop a higher appreciation for sounds of a melodic nature, expand our verbiage, and create a sound-friendly environment. Listen up and sound off!

Reflections:

Mrs. Crosbey was our librarian all through elementary school. For six years, we visited the library once a week to listen to her read, and then we would choose one book to check out. While we sat cross-legged on the floor, she sat in her chair with a drawstring bag. The bag was the home of a puppet: Oscar the badger, with a door and flower box painted on the front. When Oscar came out, some of us gave him plastic bracelets taken from gallon milk jugs. It was curious how he never spoke to us, but he whispered in her ear if he wanted to share something (his shyness was a great tactic for getting us settled in and ready to listen). The story itself was a highlight for me, as I loved how

Mrs. Crosbey transported us into the setting by altering her voice to suit characters, events, and the overall emotion of unfolding lines. It truly was a youth mini vacation.

Once I began my work with children, I carried on this tradition of keeping the little ones engaged with stories, which I read with exaggerated expression and sometimes the use of puppets. I occasionally scanned the group to see their reaction, and it was always a classic. Mouths hanging open, sparkling eyes, and giggles were perfect indicators that they had left the classroom and became part of the pages.

Journal:

Describe a story you heard or read in your youth. What in the story "clicked" for you, and how did you apply it to your learning, play, or creations? To the best of your memory, draw your favorite scene and explain why it sharpened your curiosity or made you smile (or any other reactions you experienced emotionally). How can you use past and future stories by actively applying them to daily life-if even only one small chapter?

Hands on Senses:
Once you complete your journal entry, pick up a copy of the book at the library or bookstore. I still keep a collection of my favorites and read them when I want to cheer up, need new ideas, or just want to share them with my son.

Find a quiet place to read the book out loud, with expression (record it if possible). Observe your feelings as you travel to *back when.*

Return to your journal and compare what you originally wrote to what you just read and experienced. Did the plot play out as you recalled? Are there similarities between you and a character? What do you like about the setting? Is there a message in the story you relate to? Why was it your favorite *back when?* Read the story once a week (or listen to your recording: there's quite an effect when you hear your voice and discover hidden theatrical talents).

Here's a list of audio books narrated by fun and interesting celebrities (some are masters of being childishly funny, and others are more parent-like):

- *Pecos Bill,* adapted by Brian Gleeson, read by Robin Williams

- *Frances' Audio Collection,* by Russell Hoban, read by Glynis Johns

- *Mahalia Mouse Goes to College,* by John Lithgow and Igor Oleynikov

- *Micawber,* by John Lithgow and C. F. Payne

- *Marsupial Sue,* by John Lithgow and Jack E. Davis

- *Rabbit Ears Treasury of Animal Stories: How the Rhinoceros Got His Skin, How the Camel Got His Hump, How the Leopard Got His Spots, Monkey People,* by Rabbit Ears, read by Jack Nicholson and Danny Glover

- *Victor Vito and Freddie Vasco,* by Laurie Berkner

These are must-haves as genuine smile starters! The wonderful thing about children's books is that they stimulate our vision (literally and spiritually), hearing, and positive emotions, and validate the art of pretending (dramatic play) at any age.

Passion Transistor

Reflections:

My grandparents used to buy old boxes of junk, clean the items, and sell them as another person's treasure at the flea market. When I saw Gramps walk in with the boxes, which smelled like five years of dust, he could not put them down fast enough. Grams would smile as I rummaged through the items. I think she was entertained by my enthusiasm, as she recognized the grand scavenger hunt preying on my curiosity. There was only one thing that I wanted to find every time ... transistor radios! They came in different shapes, colors, and sizes. I had quite a collection, and each one's personality seemed to induce my nightly ritual of choosing one to secretly place under my pillow to fall asleep with. The volume had to be just right so no one else could hear, and my favorite AM station played classical until around one o'clock in the morning (I knew this since I awoke when the music stopped, and I looked at my glow-in-the-dark watch).

One night, I accidentally turned the volume up in my sleep, and my grandmother instructed me to leave the radio off at night. She also advised me of how many batteries I had gone through recently. I felt a little panicked about being restricted from my lullabies and the thought of running out of batteries. My solution was to do more chores around the house to cover the cost of the batteries. My uncle took me to the store one weekend and told me I could pick out a toy. This was my opportunity to keep my bedtime fix with an ear phone, and I took it!

I love all music. Yet, back then falling asleep and dreaming that I was playing one of those classical instruments completely enchantment me and brought contentment to my heart (even with the subtle hints of occasional static). Imagine how pleased I am with the quality of sound we have today.

Journal:

How many forms of music are you well versed in? Do you listen to only one type such as rock, hip hop, jazz, or country? For each day of the week, try listening to a different genre. In your journal, include your thoughts and emotions, and why you do or do not like them. Keep an open mind and do not base your opinions on stereotypes from parents, friends, the media, or other influences. You know, the stuff like "Rock is for stoners, R&B is for thugs, country is for okey dokey pardners." Get past all that and *really* listen to the various instruments, melodies, and singers (the words have meaning too, but experience the entire song).

Nate and I take turns playing the morning DJ in our home, and it's a blast when we have time for an air guitar session with Jimi Hendrix, dance a waltz to Tomaso Albinoni, or get down with Muddy Waters. Sing, dance, and live it up!

Hands on Senses:

A local Colorado band, the Nocturnal Tomatoes, is one of the best groups that I've seen. They really know about audience participation and what entertainment is all about. Their sound is appealing, even to those who don't listen to rock, and children can't sit still when they hear the tunes. Below is a picture from a highlight in their show and should easily lead you into this activity. Remember the music you checked out during journal time? Well, now it's time to extend the experience.

www.TheNocturnalTomatoes.com

They give a new meaning to the term "You rock!" with any chosen instrument.

- Go to a local music store and explore the instruments.

- Ask to hold a guitar, sit at a piano or drums, and notice the details of the wind instruments.

- You may think, "I'm no musician." It's okay if you're not. But how does it feel to see, listen, or hold an instrument, waiting to release something that causes reactions of all types in people of all walks of life? Look at their beautiful designs, and think of what the inventor put into such a tool. Did he know how he was helping to shape the future of music?

- Everyone has a favorite instrument they love to hear. What are your top three?

- Realistically, what would stop you from trying to learn the basics of playing one of those instruments? I'm not suggesting you play on a professional or expert level. But I would suggest trying for the sake of developing a closer understanding and connection with music you hear.

- If you cannot even imagine taking lessons, at least buy a set of drumsticks and try the following:

- As every kid knows, the kitchen is the most accessible place for percussion instruments of all kinds. If you forgot the sticks, go to the kitchen anyway.

- Take out the wooden spoons in place of the drumsticks, along with everything you suspect will provide a different sound.

- Lay them out so you have easy access to them all and turn on your favorite music.

- Listen to the rhythm of the music and wait for an opening to add a new sound (no need to bang unless you have the urge to release tension without concern for your neighbors).

- Try it out on a few songs and have fun.

You next best option to this experiment is to hit the toy store and consider a xylophone, maracas, tambourine, keyboard, guitar, or *something*. At this point, forget about others seeing you as immature (it's not your fault they don't know how to have fun learning about the musical arts).

Marissa Madrid

Beautiful Brains

Reflections:

I didn't want to draw out the following account because I promised you I wouldn't focus on negative things. The point I hope you find is that everything we need to survive, even in extreme challenges, is all in the brain (or rather the mind), and there are many ways to strengthen it.

On January 18, 2002, I successfully had a brain tumor surgically removed. I never really thought much about that part of me until the neurologist informed me about the invading tumor (and showed me the MRI visuals), which had caused me grief for twelve years. At the moment that blow was delivered, I expected the doc to tell me I had a month to live ... or something more devastating than the simple fact that it was even there. But here's how it went as she pointed it out on the MRI:

"See this here, in the center. It doesn't belong there. It's a mass known as a meningioma."

GULP! "You mean a *tumor*?"

"It's a slow, growing, benign *mass*. Now you don't have much to worry about, and you shouldn't obsess over it. I consulted with my team, and there is no cause for immediate surgery."

On my way out to the parking lot, I lost it and mentally expressed a few choice words to that BLEEP. I regained my composure and went back to work, attempting to cope by turning it into something light-hearted as I explained the details to my boss. When I walked in, she could tell by my expression that something wasn't right.

"Sooo. Yeah. I have this thing in my brain ... what the doctor called a *mass*. So let me put my head in this chair and take a load off my *mass*." She wasn't very amused, and then I broke down again. Another one of my colleagues, my friend Trudy, walked in on the emotional situation and immediately asked our boss for a couple of hours off so she could take me somewhere to calm down. Our boss graciously agreed, and Trudy took me to a nail salon. I was dazed, and she offered to treat me to a manicure. I requested the massage chair instead. I can't remember what we discussed but I do know we were our crazy selves, as our somewhat unusual humor was tossed back and forth. We returned a couple hours later; my supervisor insisted that I pick up Nate from his class and then head home for downtime.

I followed her advice, and my little guy instinctively knew something wasn't right with Mama. I buckled him in the car, and he threw his arms around my neck, pulling me into a hug of infinite love. He then touched my cheek and said, "I'm here, Mama." That was phase one of digging my heels in and contemplating a successful comeback.

A few weeks later, I flipped over a bench and lost partial vision; my regular physician referred me to another team of neurologists at Denver University (cue the background miracle choir). They took one look and decided to go in and operate as soon as possible. Once past my brain pan, they discovered the invader had started to wrap around my optic nerves, leading to an additional two hours under the knife. By my standards, those who tended to me are the best team I have ever known! Talk about gratitude!

The entirety of this episode from diagnosis to complete healing actually occurred over a span of nine months, starting in June 2001. What I didn't know was that I had prepared myself with what I call *advanced healing* long before I was sedated for the procedure. Once I had a grip the second week of knowing, I researched endlessly to be better educated and to be prepared. I had many reasons to survive everything that came my way. I met no obstacles in finding a "why"; failure wasn't an option. First, I was a single mother, and no way would I miss seeing the stupendous man Nate would grow up to be. And let me add that children have the wonderful ability to cope with things when you prepare them with optimistic facts of healing physically and emotionally. Second, I was not finished with my work, which I hoped would someday inspire many. Third, I knew—with everything that I was, in that moment—that I would survive as a part of the inspiration to others as a beginning to the second "why." I embraced what I saw as a tool to empower individuals with, including four-year-old Nate. It's kind of strange ... to think that I was grateful for the lopsided brain invader.

A timid person is frightened before a danger, a coward during the time, and a courageous person afterward.
—Jean Paul Ritcher

Journal:

What are some things we can do to promote strength and development in our brain? A few that come to mind are: eat healthy, avoid toxins, and read for more knowledge. How about if we explore the brain itself (in layman's terms) for possibilities we aren't aware of?

Check out these brain facts: members.shaw.ca/hidden-talents/brain/113-maps.html

Come up with playful ideas on how you can *feed* and expand your mind from the auditory sense. Write the ideas down, implement them, and see what happens in a few weeks when you consistently feed your brain.

Hands on Senses:

With my emotions being grounded in the second week of knowing, I took things to a more scientific level and determined that if I nourished different parts of my brain, I'd be ahead in the recovery department. I researched studies and information on what could give me an edge. I think I had convinced myself that I would use every possible angle (which made sense to me) to get it right. In light of the specific concept of listening in this chapter, I will focus on that expansion. This is such a broad area of interest that I have shared my top three favorites.

- One of the first things I grounded myself with was meditation and visualizing my defeat of all obstacles. I used Kelly Howell's *Guided Meditation* CD. I had such wonderful results with the first one that I have acquired quite a few more since. I encourage you to take time in viewing her site, which includes scientific reports and explanations of how different sounds affect the brain: www.brainsync.com: Brain Wave Therapy.

- Do not underestimate this next site for youth and children only. The same concepts we use to help them applies to us adults as well. Valuable resources and tools are found throughout the site. If you're a parent, this can give your children an edge on their education (which you can share together). Every person has their own learning style, and you can provide a variety of materials for auditory processing. Some of my favorites in my classroom were signing, pictures, and changing the rhythm or sounds to words (another fun activity): www.brainadvance. com: Advanced Learning & Development Institute

- Michael Gelb, an internationally renowned author, speaker, and consultant, is a great inspiration, and his work reinforces all artistic, intellectual, and scientific pursuits. Regardless of what challenges I encounter, I always find use of his extraordinary book *How to Think Like Leonardo da Vinci: Seven Steps to Genius Every Day*. Within this masterpiece, you will find a practical approach to concepts of the senses (which I'm obviously passionate about) and ways of embracing the art of life itself. In addition to the book, try this on for the full effect of breathing in the work of the historical masters: *Musical Companion to How to Think Like Leonardo Da Vinci*: www. michaelgelb.com.

Hint: It's a given that we all hit relentless moments in our days. My suggestion is to keep a music source accessible at all times with your favorite music. Burn a CD, download your most curing songs to the MP3 player, or use any other media you have. Even just five minutes of your theme song is a worm hole to relaxing, joy, and just feeling better. Avoid commercials and other interruptions, which may add to the mental clutter of the noise that led to your stress or anxiety in the first place.

Marissa Madrid

Verbiage Value

Reflections:

I felt secure in the years leading up to junior high school, as I had attended the same elementary school since kindergarten. I had never been aggressive and walked a little on the shy side. The transition to changing classes, unfamiliar faces, and the cliques all dwarfed a part of my confidence. I sat in the first row of Mrs. Roberts's choir class, which gradually eased my doubts. We started the first week in her class with reading music and other fundamentals. My first impression of her hasn't changed, even now. I still use the image of her when I need a swift kick into action. Most others described her as a "mean old lady." My memory of her is a cultured, elegantly dressed, tall and well-postured, walking-with-a-purpose, proud of her culture, eloquent WOMAN. Not lady, W-O-M-A-N. I can hear her roar and see her fingers aggressively submit the piano into her servant of chords … wrapping us all into her one mission of teaching music with meaning.

One Monday changed me for life (Beethoven's *Symphony No. 5* was the background theme music). Mrs. Roberts began this drill session of hair-raising standards.

"Madrid! Open your mouth when you sing!"

I thought I would die from embarrassment and lose my contented spirit to a badgering hell. No one had ever caught my attention with such deliberate force. She then keyed us sopranos in again.

Her eyeballs pierced me as I opened my mouth wider, with not much more sound coming forth. I believe it was then that she recognized the expression on my face as fear. Not fear derived from singing wrong, but fear of her reaction. She abruptly stopped playing the piano and looked at me with a tad more softened expression. The mother tigress then scooted over on her bench, patted the open spot next to her, and said, "Marissa, come here, baby. You two girls behind her, come down too and stand there."

We followed as she played the tune from the book and began to sing along. She occasionally stopped to redirect one or all of us. My comfort grew as I sat next to her, feeling nurtured, and through the song, I began to understand her vision and mission of being there. This was her passion, and she would fight for it until her last breath. The woman accepted her calling and passed it on to and through us. In just that instant, I felt myself cross a threshold into the evolution of maturing as a confident young lady. On a later date, I heard her explain to someone, "If I say open your mouth, I mean let it out!" I made it a point to enroll in her class the next two years.

Being a tomboy, I give this powerful teacher props for shaping a portion of the maternal side in me. "Madrid" learned of a desire to nurture the individual needs of children. Just a couple of years ago, I saw her again, and I had no other reaction than to flood my face with tears. I shared with her what an influence she had been on my life and that I carried a love and well-wishes for her always. As the solid sculpture of grace and poise that she will always be, she hugged me with a silent smile-which needed no explaination.

Encouraged people achieve the best; dominated people achieve second best; neglected people achieve the least.
—Anonymous

Journal:

Remember all the cool words that made you accepted by your peers? You know, "That's fresh!" now interpreted as "That's phat!" My teens down at the community center will inform me that I'm still behind the times, but you get it.

Words are beautiful! Let's take a look at how many you have recently learned, let alone added to your active communication. Pick one word a day for the week and add it to your journal with an example of how or where you will use it.

Words are fun! My friend Jesse tends to point out which ones I consistently use as favorites. Listen to their sound. Then, find out what they sound like in another language. What is their origin? Try these Web sites for fun:

- Translator: babelfish.altavista.com

- Origins: www.word-detective.com/backidx.html

- Trivial facts: www.corsinet.com/trivia/j-triv.html

Hands on Senses:

What are words without music? Some songs begin as poems or stories of a person's life. Imagine if all of those boring textbooks from kindergarten though college were in the format of songs. After all, the first part of letter recognition begins as a song: "A, B, C, D, E, F, G ..."

Pick one concept or subject you would like to learn about. You can even buff up your study skills for a test.

- Pick the main concept of what you want to learn.

- Take the words or sentences and write them in an order that seems to *flow* for you.

- Now take a simple song and replace the original lyrics with what you wrote on the paper (e.g., "A, B, C, D, E,F, G, Astronomy is actually simple to me. All the stars are made from gas, with such knowledge this test I will pass ...").

Sounds goofy? Who cares? You did it as a kid to poke fun or create your own tunes. Combine the two and you have learning magic in your grasp.

Literacy, music, and comprehension: www.edu-cyberpg.com/Literacy/whatresearch5.asp

It's Not What You Hear

Reflections:

Every day, we hear the words, "How are you today?" Common courtesy is the typical intention behind the question. After I defeated the brain invader, my perception of these exchanges changed. Now instead of reciprocating with "Fine" or "Okay," I use the opportunity to challenge the person's way of thinking. My answer has now become, "I'm splendid! I woke up today!" in attempt to deliver a message of being grateful for each day and each breath I take.

To complain about the little things that will not matter one year, one week, or even five minutes later serves absolutely no purpose. When I ask the question and receive complaints, I always try to counteract the person's negative response. It may play out like this, with my initiation:

"Good morning! How are you doing?"

"Well, my boss came to work in a bad mood and chewed me out for something I didn't do. I hate this job!"

"I don't know the details of what happened, but I do know I have seen you do a great job, and I appreciate your effort. Look at it this way ... you woke up this morning with a world full of options. No day is ever better than the next or previous one to make a solid decision. The simple fact that you realize what you *don't* want is a good start to focusing on more of the good things you *do* want. I usually think of things that make me feel happy; like Nate and me creating endless laughing moments, a song, or anything to jazz things up. Have a wonderful day! It's yours!"

Usually the next time I speak with that person, they seem to have an awareness of my rejection to complaints, and they seek good things to share.

Journal:

Have you ever noticed that when something is troubling you, another person says or does something that gives you an instant eureka? You know, when you think, "That's it!" I personally believe nothing happens without a reason. Those answers and solutions hidden beneath the surface are like little treasures waiting to be uncovered. Sometimes, we look too hard or don't even pay attention. Is it a reasonable theory that if we did more active listening, we might just acquire more than delight in the conversation?

Think about some of the sayings and advice you heard when you were growing up. Did you actively listen, retain the message, and apply it in your approach to life? Think of parents and other adults who shared words of wisdom.

Write down your favorite one-liners (only encouraging and positive ones) and describe how some of your choices were influenced by them.

Hands on Senses:

I have listened to and read some the most life-impacting words of wisdom from family, friends, colleagues, and especially children. I pay close attention to the words of little ones because what they share has no limits. They do not yet base their opinions on social acceptance.

Check out a book or look online for inspirational quotes and find a favorite one. Or use one shared with you by someone. The mission in this activity is to find a personal motto that encourages you to actively pursue any and all of your goals. When you read it, it should send out the message: "I have no excuses to not try my best, and I am worthy of the results I want."

Print or write it on decorative paper with glue glitter or something eye catching. Place an adhesive magnet on the back of the paper. Last, put it on the fridge in your clear view. Below I have included a few quotes I've heard over the years that still influence my decisions today:

- "Pretty is as pretty does."—Grams (No, she didn't know Forrest Gump's mother.)

- "Toleration is the same as procrastination."—Linda Battle

- "A real man never just sits on the pot."—Gramps

- "You can never say the wrong thing to the right person."—Bruce Nelson

- "Treat the earth well: We do not inherit the earth from our ancestors; we borrow it from our children."—American Indian proverb

A principal asked Nate when he was eight years old, "What do you want to be when you grow up?" Wide eyed, Nate replied, "A good man." Bingo! I knew at that moment with no doubt, he received my messages well.

Quotes I've shared with him that may have led to that response:

- "For every question you ask, the answer is always in the mirror."

- "Titles do not express who you are, but your actions do."

- "Worry not about how to reach destiny; it becomes part of you through following your passions."

- "People with the 'show me' mentality usually have little or no faith in themselves and base decisions on fear. That fear cannot live within you without your permission. And you do not need permission to succeed."

- "Honor me with these three things: Choices that keep you and others safe, actions which make you proud and inspire others, and by doing what you love to make the world a better place."

Marissa Madrid

Nate with Sensei West at Denver
Kendo Demonstration

Refuse the battle of wits with the unarmed.
Shakespeare

Feeling of Life

Here is the place we come to literally get in touch with creatively thinking and stimulating yet another sense. Though I am fond of all senses, this one brings things to life for me. Memorization by viewing compelling graphics is wonderful to the eye, but it leaves me wanting to be in the picture. Hearing melodic sounds that I feel to the core of my spirit creates imaginative worlds, and again beckons me to be a part of that realm, where I want to be. What is your favorite?

Every individual varies in their reactions and preferences to the senses. In this section, you are encouraged to experiment soothing, relaxing, and entertaining ways to experience the tactile world.

Reflections:

My Uncle Pete took me to a carnival when I was around three. It's kind of funny how I know that we were there for a while … and yet I only recall one brief moment of it all. We went to this booth where I saw the most beautiful teddy bear. My uncle observed my reaction to the stuffed animal and made it his priority to win it for me. He paid the man for three tries at knocking bottles down with tennis balls. My guess is that maybe the tennis balls were too light, since my uncle paid for three tries again, and again, and again.

His determination brought a new best friend to me. As we were leaving the carnival, I was thinking of a name for the bear. By the time we reached the car, I declared him as my Ricky Bear. We drove home fourteen miles west to Valdez, a little mining town in southern Colorado. This was a most delightful drive, as Ricky and I felt the soft summer breeze carried through the window, drifting us into what I previously dreamed of.

That dream began a short time before when Gramps and I watched a television documentary about grizzly bears. Though they aren't of the same docile nature as Ricky, I had grasped the concept of their life cycle, somewhat. At three years old, I understood them to be fierce protectors of their cubs, leisurely eating berries, fishing in the water, hibernating, and scratching their backs on trees. Their life seemed simple and appealing, as did their thick cuddly fur and pouty bottom lips.

Onto Ricky I projected this image of the protector from thunder, cuddling companion, and the one I secretly shared snacks with.

Journal:

Softness as when held by someone you love cannot be surpassed. Is there something that you recall to be the best thing to hold, feel, and touch? Certain fabrics, Play-Do, Silly Putty, a favorite toy, a puppy, and so on. Write down whatever comes to mind. Describe the textures and why they appeal to you. Try switching it up with new descriptive words like the following:

Cottony

Cozy

Cushiony

Cushy

Delicate

Doughy

Downy

Feathery

Fleecy

Fluffy

Formless

Furry

Gelatinous

Moldable

Mushy

Pliable

Satiny

Silken

Silky

Marissa Madrid

Smooth

Snug

Spongy

Squashy

Squishy

Hands on Senses:

Explore your options of fabrics that feel nice and add a little luxury to life. Here are a few suggestions:

- Visit the fabric store and take your time running your fingers over the different textures (patterns and color sometimes add to the effect). After you pick one that feels right to your taste, purchase enough to make something. This doesn't have to be anything fancy: a small pillow, a throw blanket, or just a small piece to have on your night stand for the end-of-the-day meditation (the same principle of a worry stone).

- Try the toy department for something cuddly (don't forget to name it!).

- Treat yourself to a new set of linens (one of my favorites is sateen).

Marissa Madrid

Washed Away

Reflections:

The first time I went to a beach was an interesting experience. I naturally love the water, and as a kid I spent plenty of hours in a sandbox. This was a *tad* different, though. Growing up in Colorado is quite the contrast to a California beach.

Seventeen-year-olds are at that phase in life of thinking they are invincible, just as I did—at least until I saw the never-ending waves and countless grains of sand. The force of the waves and what they effortlessly carried in and out amazed me. I held my composure well in front of my friends to be cool, but the five-year-old in me wanted to say, "Look how vast the waves are! Oooh, look at that sand castle!" New senses in a new world of motion are too wonderful: the smell of the water, the sound of the waves, the feel of a salty mist, and the vision of nature's painterly masterpiece. As if this wasn't enough, I walked into the surf to experience the sensation of the waves crashing into me and then pulling away the sand from beneath my feet. I never knew such a joy to simultaneously experience all five senses: a powerful memory induced by the massive environment surrounding little me.

Journal:

I'm certain many other locations and events can positively affect all your senses at once. Perhaps I was so impressed with this one because of its size. Think of an ideal place you would like to visit where all of your senses are heightened. Do some light research on the location and describe how what you learned fits in with you desire to go there.

Example: www.tuscany.org/

Hands on Senses:

This one should be easy enough for anyone who likes to build, play, create, and get back to earthly inspiration.

1. Destination: toy department.

2. Required tools: sand toys. If it's out of season, try old plastic containers or something creative.

3. Call up a friend and meet at the park, beach, or wherever there is sand (a lake may work too).

4. Spend a little time digging, molding, and building your ideal place, described earlier in the journal. If present, restless natives (children) may invite themselves to your special place, so play nice if they accidentally knock down your creation.

Grandma's Hands

Reflections:

During my teens, I suffered a great deal from headaches, and not much helped (keep in mind, I had no idea this was when my mass started its invasion). Thank God for Grams! One day, I stayed home from school, crying due to this pain that showed no mercy. I could see her anxiety as she scrambled to call the doctor. She gave me a cold washcloth and told me to put it on my forehead. No results from that attempt. She tried to comfort me with words: "We are taking you for an appointment at noon." I thought, "I'll be dead by then! That's in three hours!"

I tried to muffle my woes with my pillow because seeing her worry made me feel worse. Then, she came to my side and sat down on the edge of the bed. I felt her pulling the pillow away, and she put her hand behind my neck to lift me slightly forward. Once she felt the pillow was in place, our eyes met, and I saw such strength in her eyes. She began to rub my head with her coarse, warm hands. "It's okay. I know. Shhh." She continued rubbing my head, and when I occasionally opened my eyes, I could see her praying. The pain decreased a bit, and within minutes I had fallen asleep.

She's ninety-one now. When I see her hands and fingers struck by years of labor, I wish I could return the same healing to her. I admire that she is still so independent, and when I hold those little hands in mine, I know Midas had nothing on her.

Marissa Madrid

Journal:

Seasons and weather are an everyday means to our temperature sensitivity. List the four seasons along with what you associate with their typical forecasts.

Hint: There can be some hidden poems or short stories in this one.

Hands on Senses:

Pamper yourself with seasonal care packages. Here are ideas for each season; not all items have to be purchased at once ... but they are a great inspiration for gift baskets.

- Spring: This is the season of new beginnings and warmer weather. A time for rebirth of flowers and trees; new life around you and me. Get inspired with this list!

  As You Think by Marc Allen

  A shirt or blouse (a feel-good fabric) with your new color for the year

  A small pot, soil, and seeds to plant

  A disposable camera for pictures of your growing plants

- Summer: Hello, hot sun and a time to play. Picnics, swimming, and a few vacation days.

  The Alchemist by Paulo Coelho

  Misty Mate Deluxe Personal Mist Air Cooler

  A set of sand toys

  A disposable camera for your sand creations

- Autumn: Leaves turn vibrant colors before our eyes and then fall to our feet to dry. The air is crisp on my face; these are my favorite days.

  The Four Agreements by Don Miguel Ruiz.

  A soft sweater.

  A new flavor of tea and a mug.

Wax paper and colored leaves: stretch out a piece of the paper and fold in half, place leaves in the middle, carefully insert inside a heavy book, and wait until they dry. The leaves are pretty framed or placed in a scrapbook collage.

- Winter: Ice on windows and swirling snow. Awake in the morning with a snowman to grow.

  The Blue Day Book by Bradley Trevor Greive

  Hot Stone Massage Mini Kit

  A unique and fun winter hat … with matching gloves

Bring the camera for snow fun like angels, snowmen, sledding, snowboarding, and so on.

Empty Message

Reflections:

My third grade teacher comes to mind when I hear the word "manners." She was a stout gal with those Sophia Loren spectacles, adding to the emphasis of her facial expressions. It's difficult to miss exaggerated eyes with magnified lenses covering half a face. At this second, I am officially sitting with better posture as I recall her.

She was one of those adults who presented concepts in some drab form that, quite frankly, caused me anxiety. She explained to us (repeatedly) that it was rude if we did not sit silently, very still, and straight in our seats. I didn't want to offend her, so I tried my best.

Usually ten minutes into her lessons, *it* began. All of my peers swiftly lost focus on her monotone message. Dennis, who sat behind me, had the armpit fart sound mastered every time she turned to the chalkboard. Bill drew silly pictures of WWF champions. Others started spitball and airplane fights until she saw the shadows caused from the morning sun. Then she would flip out and lecture us, again. I thought of my previous teachers and how they included us in their lessons with challenging questions, objects we passed around for observation, and sometimes simple competitive games. I think this was a contribution to my future success in the classroom.

For my little ones who had a very short attention span, I would ask them to hold the book I read, my special Beanie Baby, a swoosh ball, or something that they could take care of during story time. Each day, I chose different children for this favor, and because each one wanted so badly to be a helper, they competed by showing great listening skills. In the end, I asked them questions about what they learned, and for each correct answer, I rewarded them by allowing them to choose a special activity or something meaningful to them. The amazing part was that these kids were in preschool. Fifteen minutes to them is a lifetime. I later learned from one of our speech therapists that letting them hold something that they could squeeze or quietly manipulate helped some of them focus better. I was so happy when my employer started doing this for us at out training meetings. It sure helped with those eye-watering, trying-not-to-yawn hours of sitting there.

Journal:

Can you say information overload, or visual and audio overstimulation? When we are children, we are often restricted from moving an inch when we are supposed to be attentive. Write down some mental blockers that sometimes trip you up when you are working, listening, or just trying to stay focused. Try the activity and suggestions below, and describe whether they helped you (and how).

Hands on Senses:

Squeeze out the stress! Whenever you make a fist, whether you hold something in your hand or not, you create muscle tension. And when you release your grip, your muscles relax. This process of acute muscle tension and relaxation can relieve stress. You can perform this stress management technique without a stress ball, by simply tensing and relaxing the muscles in your hands (or anywhere on the body that tension exists). But a stress ball gives you something to focus on and may aid in relieving stress. Stress balls have been used for years for a wide range of medicinal purposes. Stress balls were used in ancient civilizations (originally bagan as the two spheres rolled in the palm, now eveolved into the ball we know today as soft and/or squishy) to relieve stress, improve coordination, prevent arthritis, prevent rheumatism, stimulate blood circulation, help during physical therapy, and assist with meditation. Stress balls may also help prevent or treat carpal-tunnel syndrome.

Materials Needed:

Large balloons

Permanent Marker

Corn starch (salt, flour, or sand as alternatives)

Small funnel

Instructions:

1. Look for a small, thick, round balloon.
2. Blow it up until it is about four to five inches around. (Don't tie the balloon yet!)
3. Use permanent markers to draw designs or inspirational words on the balloon.

4. Release the air after your design is complete.

5. Place a small funnel inside the opening of the balloon.

6. Using the funnel, pour cornstarch into the balloon.

7. Slowly release the top of the balloon so the cornstarch can slide down.

8. Continue adding cornstarch until your balloon is about three inches in diameter.

9. Tighten the end of the balloon and slowly let out any remaining air.

10. Tie the balloon closed as near to the cornstarch as you can.

11. Squish and mold your creation, watching the designs or words curve and expand.

A bag of homemade Silly Putty is great to keep in a desk drawer.

Recipe:

This is really kind of a tricky recipe because it's like making bread. Try making it a few times to get just the right texture. Also, cheaper brands of glue may not work as well because they have too much water in them. Combine approximately two parts glue to one part liquid starch. Stir it up, and it will stick to whatever you're stirring it with. If the mixture sticks to your fingers, add more liquid starch. If it doesn't stick to itself, add more glue. Store it in an air-tight container in the fridge. If you want the mixture to get tougher and thicker, let it dry out a bit in the air. If you get it just right (and I rarely do), it will pick up newsprint like the store-bought stuff. You can also add plastic seed beads to create another texture like Floam.

Get out your cornstarch again! This is a colorful experiment for home and not a bad conversation piece during get-togethers.

Materials Needed:

- 1/3 cup sugar
- 1 cup cornstarch
- 4 cups water
- 3 tbsp food coloring for each color (red, blue, and yellow)
- 3 ziplock bags
- Tape

Instructions:

Mix together the first three ingredients in a saucepan. Stir constantly and heat until the mixture begins to thicken. Remove from heat and let cool.

- Divide the mixture into three bowls.
- Add approximately three tablespoon of each color (red, blue, yellow) into the bowls (keeping each color separate) and stir till color is consistent.
- Scoop 2 tablespoons of each color in equal parts into each bag.
- Seal the bag and tape the top closed (try not to trap air in).
- Knead the bag to mix colors just enough to look like a rainbow.
- Lay bag down on a hard surface and gently press to flatten it or simply manipulate it by squeezing the colors gently between your fingers. You can hang it in your window when finished.

Don't forget to seal the bag with tape!

Marissa Madrid

Scents of Yesteryear

You pass a restaurant, person, or something that flashes you to *back when*, with a simple whiff of the air. I'm no expert on explaining this emotional process in scientific terms, so check this site out for basic but good information:

www.macalester.edu/psychology/whathap/UBNRP/Smell/memory.html

Senses are truly a perfect design of our physical makeup, and this one can create beautiful memories. Think about it! Generally, if we smell chlorine, we may recall fun days in a pool with friends and family, not just being at a swim pool alone. Smell something baking and you may think of more than just Grandma or a favorite aunt making brownies, you may also recall the maternal icon with love.

I found a natural merging of smells and tastes, so the two senses are combined. Also, aromatherapy is often used as a sleep aid; you'll encounter more smells in the section of Scented Hills.

Setting the Table

Reflections:

A common scene at Grandma's house during holidays was a few family members gathered around the table, making tamales. Talk about a process! First the meat had to be cooked with a perfect blend of chili and spices, while the corn husks were soaked and cleaned, and the masa (doughy part) was prepared. Grams then assigned a person to the corn husks, which were patted to remove excessive moisture and then spread with the masa. The next person added the filler and rolled and folded the tamale in place. Usually Gramps was at the end, and he turned extra corn husks into ties, which held the final product together.

The spicy little presents were then steamed, and once the scent was released into the air, our tummies grumbled with the greatest desire to unwrap the first one.

We are not a tall family, so basically what you'd see is a few little Latino people in their version of Keebler elves hard at work. This all took place around an old oval table made of stainless steel, with gray Formica covering the surface (I think they bought it in the forties). *If that table could only talk*. As toddlers, all of the grandchildren have swung on its bars. The food that has been prepared on it would stretch for miles: Italian cookies, tortillas, chili and garlic ground with a *molcajete*, cakes, breads, and so much more. Keep in mind, this is a natural breeding ground for stories, jokes, and observing family members in a unique light. Now that's what I call quality time! It really hits my mind as I think about it. Our family has never had millions of dollars … but boy, are we rich in tradition, tasty food, and memories of pure love and happiness that took place around that table. An old table, $50. Tamale ingredients, $80. The memories around the old table, priceless. Gramps reupholstered the chairs once with the same blue genuine simulated leather and silver tacks. I wish I could have captured all of those delicious scents in decorative bottles for an occasional trip to *back when*. What a wonderful experience … without weight gain to top it off!

Marissa Madrid

Journal:

What if you could keep a scent in a bottle that brought joy to your heart? What would it be, and what memories are attached to it? Get to writing, and you may have an inspirational piece of work on your hands. Elaborate on the complete experience, and you'll find a way to share a part of you with others who genuinely love a great story.

Hands on Senses:

Do a little research with family members and find your favorite childhood dish. If nothing comes to mind, check out a recipe book or look online for a traditional dish to call your own. I suggest you find something that doesn't take all day, but something that requires all your senses in the process of making: textures to touch, colors of the ingredients or arrangement of food (notice when you see something that looks good, you want it more). Experiment with spices or new foods for scents, leading to the delectable taste on your tongue.

Here are a few resources:

allrecipes.com/
www.recipegoldmine.com/
www.101cookbooks.com/quick_recipes/
Recipe Hall of Fame Quick & Easy Cookbook: Winning Recipes from Hometown America (Quail Ridge Press Cookbook Series) by Gwen McKee and Barbara Moseley

Marissa Madrid

Smoke Signals

Reflections:

Parents' night had been scheduled and our theme was storybook characters. I had short hair at the time, so my supervisor informed me that I would wear the wizard hat and round lenses of Harry Potter. Not quite what I had in mind, but I played along.

One of my colleagues, a great friend, transformed her classroom into a scene from *Charlotte's Web* and asked me to draw a poster for her door. At that time of the day, there weren't any children around, so we put our time and effort to good use as our creative juices stirred. After I completed the poster of Wilbur for her, I noticed a popcorn machine over in the corner of her room. For a brief moment, I wondered why it was located by the back door ... and realized it was a good place since the building we worked in was over a hundred years old, and you'd never know if the heat from the machine would set off a fire alarm.

That night, the building became a living storybook, with all of the staff dressed in costumes. About an hour into the event, the smoke detector went off and we had to evacuate. The firefighters arrived promptly, and needless to say, the popcorn machine I observed had set off the alarm. As I stood in the playground out back and watched the smoke leaving slowly out of the window, a group of parents and children who attended the Family Night event were with me. I heard one of the small voices explain to another, "The *real* Harry Potter would waive his wand and we wouldn't be standing out here." The other kid replied, "Yeah. Don't they teach him about smoke signals?"

Once the coast was clear, we all returned to the fairy tale land of the burnt smell. My friend was embarrassed, but she handled it with such grace in her farmer costume and pigtails. I think the red bandana pulled up outlaw style was a true demonstration of her survival tactics.

Journal:

Come up with as many words as you can to describe the scents of the following items:

Roses

Pizza

Coffee

Cinnamon

Popcorn

Chocolate

Crayons

Rain

Now write who or what they remind you of and detail the environment surrounding what you remember based on the smell.

Hands on Senses:

Ever want to improve the scent of a room, a car, or maybe just a closet? Here are a few simple ideas:

- Grab an orange and a handful of cloves. Stick the cloves into the oranges. Take a small piece of ribbon and a straight pin. Loop the ribbon and stick the straight pin through it into the orange.

- Simmer a sliced lemon, grapefruit, and orange in water using an aluminum pot (covered) for one hour. This adds a fresh scent to your home and is a nice way to shine up the pot.

- Soak a few cotton balls in lemon, almond, or your favorite extract. Place them in a drawstring sachet and change as needed.

Speaking in Tastebuds

Reflections:

The only permanent side effect of my brain surgery was losing my right olfactory gland. In other words, I can only smell out of one nostril. I never would have known it until the surgeon pointed out that they had to remove it. A small sacrifice, I'd say. I am so grateful for having one left, since I love to cook, and I love the scents of various kinds of food. This makes me wonder. Would my cooking still be as sought out by family and friends if I had lost both glands, since I wouldn't be able to taste spices and seasonings? Not a risk I'm willing to take! It would be "woth than a stubt nodes"!

Journal:

List your favorite tastes and create something once a day for one week from that list. Try to keep it healthy, friends! Here's an example:

Taste	Monday	Tuesday	Wednesday	Thursday	Friday
Sweet	Apple slices w/ PB				
Sour		Ice water with lemon			
Minty			Tea with pepper-mint leaves		
Nutty				Almonds and dried apricots	
Spicy					Green salsa

Hands on Senses:

I am sworn to secrecy with some family recipes but this one is definitely an easy favorite:

Green salsa

4 servings

Ten tomatillos (looks like a green tomato covered with a dry skin in the produce section)

¼ tsp salt

1 clove garlic

3 sprigs cilantro

2 diced scallions

1 finely diced Serrano chili pepper (without stem)

Corn chips

Peel the skin off the tomatillos (most are a little larger than a golf ball) and rinse thoroughly. Combine first four ingredients in a blender and blend until tomatillos are in sauce form. Mix in scallions, pepper, and additional salt to taste. Grab the corn chips and enjoy! Note: Some people claim that cilantro tastes like soap; just an observation of the unique individual senses out there.

Marissa Madrid

Colors of Us in Cultural Foods

Reflections:

Coming from that line of hard-working Latino Keebler elves, our tradition of good food was not just for the sake of flavor and satisfaction. Nutrition has always been of the highest priority, where the men know how to sew and women aren't strangers to pouring a slab of cement.

My grandparents emphasized the importance of a solid breakfast to sustain mental awareness and the start of endurance for any task. As for how I view nutrition now, it is a bit more spiritual in the way of gratitude for having daily essentials and the artistic approach of the fact that *we are what we eat.*

Ah … food. The variety has such an appeal in artistic presentation. Melodies of fruits and veggies grown from Mother Earth, as she nurses them with water, minerals, and vitamins. Wheat, rice, and grains yield another source of our body's needs. Milk, butter, and cheese from another animal who shares life with us through iron and calcium to strengthen muscles, bone, and tissue. Think of the perfect orchestration between bountiful food and how it chisels the human body into the ultimate sculpture.

To equal the variety of food, there are many types of diets. My personal theory is that what you eat is not as important as how much you eat. I know that when I'm the mastermind of my kitchen, I focus on combining the beautiful array of culture, colors, taste, and textures … a reflection of what I would like to be. Cultural dishes are a valuable way to experiment with the history of the fine art. Excess isn't my goal, but eyeing a balanced meal with the assortment of abundance is my mission (including light snacks).

Journal:

If you could be any entrée, presented on fine dinnerwear, what would you be? I know this may sound odd to some, but think of it this way: Most of America is obsessed with diet, society's expectations, and how we look in the mirror. When I look in the mirror, it's not difficult to recognize that extra burger hanging onto a bulky hip or thigh. If my goal was to look like that burger with sauce and other stuff seeping out the sides, I'd glutton-size every meal … with an illegal-sized side of cellulite enhancer, of course.

See yourself as sweet with a bit of twang? Try a fruit salad with freshly squeezed lemon juice.

Feeling hot and spicy? Dip into the salsa recipe I shared earlier.

See your body as the masterpiece you want it to be. Replace lumps and bumps with smooth and strong contours by matching results you want to see with the natural lines and colors of food. Create a list of seven foods you want to add to your diet for the week (start with small snacks). Remember to bump the junk stuff with these newbies. Savor and indulge with each bite, focusing on how your palate is more satisfied with healthier ways of eating.

Examples (not sure about amounts? Use serving size information on the package.):

Monday	Tuesday	Wednesday	Thursday	Friday	Saturday	Sunday
Blueber-ries/ ½ bagel	Cream cheese/ wheat crackers	Carrots/ ½ apple	Grapes/ mild cheddar cheese	Toast/ ½ or-ange	Creamy Swiss cheese/ almonds	Create your own salad

Hands on Senses:

Here are some recipes and suggestion to connect with the concept of remolding a healthier you. You may have restrictions or allergies, so please keep in mind this is solely for the purpose of inspiring others to embrace healthier eating concepts (and a means to embrace nutrition).

Salads: the elements that make up chlorophyll in plants and the elements that make red blood cells are nearly the same. Chlorophyll cleanses, heals, and builds the human body cells.

Why salads as a snack or meal? Three commonsense reasons:

- They are quick and easy to make.

- Salads go with anything and anything can go on salads i.e.: nuts, fruit, cheese, etc.

- Salads fit any budget with room for fish, meats, or what ever you crave

My top three favorite salads:

Kidney Bean Salad

4 servings

1 cup drained can of kidney beans

1 orange or 2 small Clementine oranges, peeled and sectioned

½ red onion, sliced in rings

½ celery stalk, thinly sliced

½ green and red bell pepper, diced

½ cup of walnuts, pine nuts, or your favorite kind of nut

In a small bowl, mix the following:

1 tbsp rice, red wine, or apple cider vinegar

½ lime, freshly squeezed

1 tsp honey

1 tsp olive oil

Combine all ingredients, gently folding in the dressing. Chill and serve (you can line bowls with large lettuce leaves for extra eye appeal).

Fruit Salad

4 servings

½ cup blueberries

½ cup grapes

½ cup strawberries, sliced

1 cup Mandarin oranges

1 peach, sliced

2 cups cottage cheese

Mix all the fruit. Line four bowls with ½ cup of cottage cheese.

In a small saucepan, combine the following:

2 tbsp honey

¼ cup raspberry jam
Juice of 1 lemon

Blend ingredients on low setting until consistency is caramel like. Pour over top of fruit and serve.

Salad Festivo

4 servings

1 can Mexican corn, drained

½ Boston lettuce head, torn

1 small zucchini, sliced

1 tomato, wedged

½ red bell pepper, diced

½ cup sunflower seeds

Mix ingredients, chill.

Dressing:

3 tbsp lemon juice

2 tsp olive oil

½ tsp cilantro, finely chopped

½ tsp honey

1 garlic clove, finely chopped

¼ tsp cayenne pepper

⅛ tsp salt

Mix and pour evenly over salad, serve.

Traditional Taste

Reflections:

In settings where family-style meals are served to children, many lessons are learned. When you mix up the diverse backgrounds and traditions of children, many conversations come to light. The children in my class would share what they ate the night before or over the weekend. One conversation I fondly recall took place between several three to five year old kids of different ethnicities:

"My mom made McDonald's. After that, we had popcorn and watched this movie about lizards that ate bugs with their tongue."

"Hey! I ate bugs one time when we were in Mexico!"

All the kids responded in shock: "Eeewwww!"

"What? They were good!"

"My mom would be scared in that kitchen cause all she makes is pork chops and potatoes and stuff like that."

"My dad makes us real hot chili and we use tortillas for scoops. It's so good."

"Guess what? When we go to my grandma's in California, we eat sushi. Did you know that's fish that they don't cook?"

I took this opportunity as a learning moment for us all and created a lesson plan with nutrition, cultural traditions and their history, and the opportunity for parents to exchange recipes. Once I started researching the history of foods and their origins, this added to my passion for cooking new dishes. My family looked at me like I had lost my mind on occasion; not knowing what was on the table. After they got past trying something different, content tummies and praise followed.

Journal:

Not ever being a picky eater, I was always open to trying something new. Thank goodness Nate has the same open mind. After witnessing children as young as three only wanting one thing to eat, I wondered how they would meet other of challenges in life.

Pick a favorite meal and explore where the ingredients to that meal originated. You may discover you are eating foods from different parts of the world. Briefly tell what you learned; how can you expand your geographical food experience by adding just one new ingredient to your existing selection? I know we don't have enough time to spend on too many trivial details. But think of the abundance of all those little details at our fingertips!

Hands on Senses:

Start with your journal entry. From there, find a recipe (or use one you have on hand). This one is a little on the indulgent side, but rich in history and culture.

Date Coconut Balls

8 servings

½ stick of butter

½ cup brown sugar

1 pack of dates

1½ cups of Rice Krispies

1 cup coconut in a ziplock bag

Combine first 2 ingredients in a saucepan and heat on low and stir until there is a candied appearance. Add the dates, stir well. Last, add the Rices Krispies and stir till all is coated with the candied mixture. Remove from heat and cool. Once the mixture is cool enough to handle, roll the mixture into balls. Individually drop the balls into the bag of coconut and gently shake until well covered. Place them on a plate covered with wax paper and chill in the refrigerator for one hour.

History, science, and culture in the recipe:

- Dates: Believed to have originated in the Persian Gulf; archaeological traces of cultivation in Arabia begin around 4000 BC.

- Nutrition facts: www.thefruitpages.com/chartdates.shtml

- Rice Krispies: What's that sound? Better yet, what's the science behind it? Find out on this site: www.livescience.com/environment/060424_MM_rice_krispies.html

- Butter: Can be traced back to 9000 BC; originally derived from sheep and goat milk.

- Brown sugar: A mixture of refined sugar and molasses.

- Coconuts: Believed to have originated in either South Asia or South America.

A Time to Move and Move Your Role!

Many of the concepts I have shared with you so far are soothing, therapeutic, and light in activity. Meditation and placid times are healthy and nurture your spirit *if* you do not pollute your mind with nothingness as you sit like a couch lump. Take a minute to think of how dynamic your body is. It was built for action, purpose, and function. You don't have to hit the gym like a professional to be fit. Being fit is as simple as doing *something* to promote movement. I never could grasp the idea of sitting on idle in front of a TV for hours, living life through its characters, while my own life was a matter of writing, stepping out the front door, or just going for a thirty-minute walk. Check out the sites in the Resources section to discover exactly how activity is crucial to our bodies, our energy, and our life. Enjoy the games!

Reflections:

In that little old mining town of Valdez, our main source of fitness activities was being out in nature. I wasn't quite running marathons at three, so Gramps and I would walk along the train tracks and beside the Purgatory River. We looked for special rocks or glass conductors that had fallen from telephone poles, anything that he had a story to match. It was our evening tradition to walk after dinner. When the snow moved in, he would still find some sort of exercise for us to join in, including rolling giant snowballs into the best snowmen. This is where I developed my love for the outdoors, which is still a way for me to spend meaningful time with my son.

Though it is no longer a nightly ritual, we sometimes extend our adventures for the entire day. Most of the terrain we choose is a natural treasure hunt for candid moments with our cameras. Whether we are at Fountain Creek Nature Center or in Cheyenne Cannon, the long walks are always rewarding physically, spiritually, and artistically. There is always so much more to show in your health and intellect when you have a fitness plan.

I didn't intend to repeat my preference of activities. This is just to reinforce that there is no excuse for not doing something: the cost, a lack of supplies and materials, or anything else. Walking out the front door is always a step in a new direction.

Journal:

Pick up a city map and lay it out on the table (or mount it on a wall as a constant visual reminder). Highlight all of the parks or nature centers that are within reasonable distance. Pick one park to visit for a couple of hours one day out of the week for one month. During each visit, pick an observation spot and write what you see in your journal. Take a walk and put your senses into overdrive. Have a friend with you? Be brave and step onto the playground. Take a swing, play in the sand, or try the monkey bars. Long ago, I assigned myself as the professional slide tester. You can also document some of the memories you recall as you play.

Hands on Senses:

If you do have a friend with you at the park, try this game. Use a scarf as a blindfold (take turns and play nice). The person who's in the dark sits on a bench while you move away. Once you have placed yourself past various obstacles like swings, tables, or another bench, you call to the blindfolded person. The object is for the blindfolded person to use their other senses to reach you. The blindfolded person should extend their hands in front as a way to feel around and to prevent them from walking into anything. You can give hints if your partner is walking toward something in the way: "Walk more to the right, Betty. There's a bush in front of you." Once you both meet up, switch the roles. This is a great team-building activity for communication, environmental awareness, and trust.

Living Out Loud

Reflections:

The school bell rang and I was the first kid out the sixth grade door. My backpack, loaded with homework and books, seemed weightless as I ran at warp speed. It almost seemed as if my feet never touched the sidewalk or the driveways that I passed to reach the back entrance to home.

Grams was cleaning the table as I cleared the three steps up to the kitchen door. She asked me in Spanish, "Marissa! What's wrong?"

I threw my backpack on the table, unzipping it with sheer excitement. In a not-so-graceful manner, I pulled a white form out.

"Grandma! Hurry, get a pen! You know that classical music I listen to all the time? Well, look! I get to see that, and guess what else? Our class is going to the Pikes Peak Center to see a ballet! Here's the permission slip you *have* to sign."

"Okay, okay, Marissa. Let me read it." She put her glasses on, sat in a chair, and began to scan the form. "Let's see here." A pause lasting all eternity silenced the room. In my mind, I thought there was nothing to read since I just explained what it was.

She laid her signature on the paper (with what I have always thought to be the most beautiful handwriting). "Here you go; don't forget to give it to your teacher. Is that where those men and women wear leotards and tutus?"

"*Yes,* Grandma. It's not until next Tuesday, so we have the weekend to go shopping."

"You have to take something?"

"No, I don't have anything to wear. I have seen in books and on TV where people always get dressed up for these things." (As a tomboy, this was the one exception I'd turn my jeans in for.)

"I don't think you have to."

"Watch!" I ran to the shelf with ancient encyclopedias and pulled out my proof of claims. Opening the book, I pointed to a picture, making my point. "See, Grams."

"We can eat leftovers when we get back. Pete, get the car started so we can go to the mall."

I thought in that moment, "God, she loves me. Thank you for allowing her to understand."

That evening, I found the perfect dress and shoes … and my first-time nylons. Wow: another turning point into becoming a young lady. When Tuesday came, I went to school, and the boys I usually played basketball and football with approached me with confused expressions. They asked why I was dressed up.

"Everyone dresses up for the ballet," I explained.

At the time, I had no idea that this was of definite sentimental value to me. I wanted the full experience of knowing what this artistic and cultural event was like (for fear that I would never have that chance again outside of school).

We sat up high, where I could see the stage in clear view with elaborate decorations and the orchestra below, in front. The performance began, and my heart was in heaven with the mind-blowing music and the talented dancers. It came to an end, and as we left, some of my friends were laughing about the guys in tights and talking about other details. I remember thinking that they just didn't understand what a classical moment we had just been exposed to. As for my reaction … I savored it all well into that night and the days that followed.

Journal:

Music is like magic. It invites us to dance, move, and experience a broad range of emotions. As mentioned earlier, some songs have verbal meanings and some have different meanings in the sense of how they make you feel. Write down four categories of emotions, like exhilarated, desolate, reposing, and vivacious. Next to each category, list some songs that create these various sensations within you. Contemplate the ways you can use those songs to put an extra step in your day, gain peace in a hectic day, or reflect on the songs that add to being mopey or lacking energy. The concept here is to get your groove (or waltz) on for the sake of exercise and action, light and heavy cardio, whether for fifteen minutes or an hour.

Hands on Senses:

Here are some of my CD recommendations for areas of inspiration, emotion, and energy:

Immediate Boosts

- *Putumayo World Music*
- *Lilo and Stitch* soundtrack
- *Shrek* soundtrack
- *Putumayo Presents: Latin Jazz*

Peace and Calm

- *Rhythmic Fission: Digital Revisions of Classic Trax*
- *The Calming Collection: Sleep Solutions*
- *Deep Stress Relief* by Kelly Howell
- *Plains* by George Winston

Inspiration

- *K-PAX* soundtrack
- *Piano Dreamers* by various artists
- **Mozart:** *Le Nozze di Figaro,* **Te Kanawa, Cotrubas, von Stade, Luxon, Skram, Fryatt; Pritchard, Glyndebourne Opera**
- *The Marriage of Figaro* Wolfgang Amadeus Mozart

Sandman Impressions and Scented Hills

Pikes Peak in March

Ah, the world of healing, rest, and rejuvenation. We pass through dreams of flight, memories, and impossibilities upon falling asleep. Trials and satisfactory events have an influence on the ascendancy of a night's untold story, which plays in our minds as clips of all genres seen in movies or read in books. This section invites you to actualize what you may need to find healthier rest and induced scenes of contentment. Here are reminiscences and suggestions to help you create your sacred place of slumber.

Marissa Madrid

Reflections:

I grew up next to the foothills near Pikes Peak, Colorado; it was covered with many forms of life. All of us neighborhood kids considered this area the best playground; we used the snowy hills for high-speed tubing, played hide-and-seek, and just lay back to watch clouds turn into faces, animals, and other things. My personal favorite memory of the hills was the scents that came to life after a good rain.

I took my dog Duke, who looked like a mammoth bear, for walks after the rain, and the scent that always made me late coming home was the dampened sage. I would do almost anything to linger in the aroma, including secretly opening my window after Grams fell asleep. I lay on my bed, breathing in the light hint of sage, and drifted like a floating feather into a deep slumber of foothill paradise.

Journal:

What are some of the scents or environmental attributes that help you find a restful night? Temperature of the room, soft sheets, soft music, or maybe the scent of your pillowcase?

Make your list, and over the next few weeks, experiment with your ideas or the suggestion in Hands on Senses. Once you figure out what works for you, make it your self-pampering habit.

Hands on Senses:

Before you use natural herbs or oils, always read about them first. This is not just for knowledge, but for respect of their use as well.

- Two drops jasmine (*Jasminum officinale*) essential oil

- Three drops Roman chamomile (*Chamaemelum nobile*) essential oil

- Four drops lavender (*Lavandula augustifolia*) essential oil

- Six drops spikenard (*Nardostachys jatamansi*) essential oil

Combine these essential oils to help with insomnia, or create your own aromatherapy recipe using the essential oils suggested for insomnia. Place a few drops on cotton pads in a sheer sachet. Place it on your nightstand or hang it on a bedpost.

Afternoon Zs

Reflections:

One day, I spent my lunch hour at school with Nate during nap time. Despite his excitement of seeing me, sleep was still an option, and he invited me to rub his back. I agreed and thought that I would leave once he started dreaming.

Soft music played, and as I stroked his dark hair, his eyes grew heavy. He in turn rubbed my arm. The first time he dozed off, he abruptly grabbed my hand to ensure that I would stay for the entire hour. I surrendered to his silent request and observed him and the other children, who all appeared like angels. Sitting cross-legged, I bent over closer to my son and held his small, warm hand on my cheek. It felt so good just to be there with him, like when he was first born. I closed my eyes and felt my head nod a couple of times; I never considered the remote possibility that I was about to crash.

Then, with a sudden knock of my head on the corner of his cot, crash was exactly what I did. I was immediately embarrassed. It was like when you are walking along and you trip, then look behind you at the ground to make it seem like you tripped over something … like it was the ground's fault. To top it off, you look around to see if anyone was watching. Once I reassured myself that no one witnessed my kiss with the cot and I didn't awaken any children, I noticed Nate had let go of my hand. I whispered, "I love you," in his ear and left quickly, but quietly.

Journal:

Sometimes, we express how nice a nap would be or wish for some other source of pleasure.

I found that yielding to some of those desires is not all bad, and sometimes we should listen to what our body requests. List three little things you would like to engage in more often. It doesn't have to be daily. Think of things that would give you an edge or increase your energy, awareness, motivation, and enthusiasm. What does your body ask for more of?

Hands on Senses:

Take time to explore all of the supporting reasons as to how and why occasional indulgences are validated. Schedule the luxuries in your calendar each week! Notice that the examples below all lead to relaxation.

Examples:

- Power nap: In Robert Fulghum's *All I Really Need to Know I Learned in Kindergarten,* number twelve on his list was *Take a nap every afternoon* (many experts agree).

- Chocolate (in moderation): Dark chocolate is high in flavonoids (an antioxidant).

- Longer baths: These can help circulation and fatigue (another opportunity for aromatherapy).

Marissa Madrid

Strategic Environment: Go Green!

How do you react to colors and placement of things? What type of environment promotes your healthy emotions and actions? Though we usually cannot change our work space, we can modify and add simple pleasures to our favorite room. Explore the possibilities of how you can make your happy place full of safety, comfort, and harmony through this section.

Reflections:

Two of the greatest environmental icons I recall are Woodsy Owl and Iron Eyes, the crying Native American character in the TV commercials. Back then, the concerns with our earth were mainly about not dumping trash out the window and not polluting our waters. I can vividly recall telling Gramps, "Ooooh, that man doesn't give a hoot! He threw that trash out the window!"

As a kid in the late seventies, we didn't know about the more devastating effects of some of our consumables. A prominent memory is when Grams cleaned the house with ammonia and other products. Opening the windows didn't prevent headaches and symptoms that I now know were caused by harsh chemicals. After doing my homework on the ingredients, I have looked back on all the times we visited the doctor, who diagnosed me with bronchitis or other respiratory infections. Is it possible the cleaning products were culprits? Maybe. Many of our parents had no idea about this. Now, we as parents can better educate ourselves in prevention measures.

For the sake of not arguing about what's good for individuals or not, I can only suggest what has worked for my family for the last couple of years. Consider the simple fact that you cannot leave a box of cleaning products or any other toxins for your trash service to haul away with other garbage. You have to take it to a special disposal site *yourself.* Now, if you sit for a second and rationally think about that, why would we have such items in our homes … and why would we not care enough to stop putting them into our environment?

I have never been much of an activist or extremist on environmental issues. I can say that my small contribution to the earth by using green products has undoubtedly improved many aspects of my family's life. For me alone, I now know that the days that I felt fatigued or gloomy are now but a distant part of my past.

Everyone has to do what's best for them. All I suggest here is to do a little research and discover if it's worth anything to you, and the earth, to try natural products compared to others. Here are just a few brief facts that you can identify with since your products labels usually give warnings to use in well-ventilated areas (I never could figure that one out, when they are meant for an enclosed restroom):

- Air freshener: Highly flammable. Health effects include irritation to the eyes, throat, and lungs. Fumes act as a nerve-deadening agent to cover up one smell with another but can be very damaging to the respiratory tract.

- All-purpose cleaner: Highly flammable. Health effects include irritation and damage to the skin, eyes, and lungs. Fumes can cause dizziness and feelings of light-headedness. Chronic irritation may occur from repeated use.

- Carpet cleaner: May contain carcinogenic and toxic fumes causing dizziness, nausea, loss of appetite, and sleepiness.

- Floor cleaner: Flammable. Fumes irritate skin, eyes, throat, mucous membranes, and respiratory tract. Inhalation causes headaches and drowsiness.

Journal:

Have you ever considered that your environment could have an impact on your well-being? Not just through the information I just provided, but others as well. A wide range of studies have shown that our environment has an influence on how we behave socially, cognitively, and emotionally. It is fair to assess how crowded children and adults respond to closed-in or cluttered spaces with anxiety, higher levels of frustration, or overstimulation of the senses. Cognition is our brain receiving information through such responses experienced by all five senses. Another example is the colors of walls and aesthetic designs connecting thoughts and emotions.

From your comfy spot at home, take a look around the room you are sitting in. Notice the walls, floor, items on tables, and so on. As you are looking, consider some of the details you would like to add, subtract, enhance, or change. Is there too much clutter, not enough visual warmth, or too many unappealing colors? How about the arrangement of furniture? Are there natural-scented candles to complement the coziness of the room?

Write about the things you want to make small changes to. Describe how this change will bring warmth to the room. This can be as subtle as clearing a few items from a shelf or moving a piece of furniture to another room (or getting rid of it altogether). Quaint flower arrangements, small plants, and potpourri are examples of tranquil little touches.

Hands on Senses:

When we initially moved into our home, I felt it was a priority to decorate my son's room first. Even with his Bruce Lee wall scrolls and other Asian decorations, the walls appeared drab and somewhat cold. Considering that he would be changing schools and going through other transitions, I wanted him to have his peaceful, quiet (but sometimes loud) place to nurture his emotional, intellectual, and educational needs. I took a week off from work, and the end result of my effort actually surprised me. What I didn't anticipate was the morning sun coming through the blinds with the appeal of warm and inviting textures I had created with faux painting. His room has become a favorite place to hang out with friends, with the feeling of being wrapped in a blanket out of the dryer on a snowy day.

After journaling some of the basic changes you'd like to make in a room of your choosing, list those details from the smallest to largest. The idea of this is not to spend a lot of money, but to open up spaces for more breathing room and small doses of stimulating your senses.

Fountain Creek Path

- Downsize items on shelves (knickknacks and papers)

- Add a plant to nurture

- Add a few candles for scent and soothing light at night and on cloudy days

- Rearrange books; expand your library of inspiring and positive literature (some coffee table books are wonderful for cleansing thoughts and ideas)

- Add a couple of pillows or blanket with different soothing colors and textures

- Rearrange the room to open up its flow

- Paint a wall with textures, or wallpaper a mural

- Add a natural-looking piece of furniture

- Hang a painting or picture that promotes your imagination and mental escape

Once your list is in the order you like, make the gradual transformation and notice how the small changes become a part of your corner of the world. Don't forget to add a piece or two that are symbolic of the creative kid in you. Need ideas for that one? No problem ...

- Table games like chess, Pylos, Quoridor, Batik, Mancala

- Brain teasers

- Decorated note/sketch pad and color markers or pencils for sudden ideas

- Mini Zen garden or meditation balls

- Bowl of smooth stones you collect on nature walks

- Kaleidoscope

- Slinky

- Modern tops

Tops, water, flashlight, mirror, and blue
construction paper…what can you create
with things found around your home?

Keep true to the dreams of thy youth.
—Friedrich von Schiller

Dreams of Paris

Reflections:

When we still lived in Valdez, Colorado, Grams had an assortment of perfumes on her dresser, some very ancient and others, new. The one I was particularly fond of was in a little cobalt blue bottle called "Evening in Paris." One morning while Grams was using the scrub board for laundry, I innocently wandered into her bedroom. Standing on my tiptoes, I grasped the bottle very quietly and carefully. A dab here and there would suffice my cause. It then occurred to me that she might notice the lower level of good-smelling liquid in the bottle. I took the bottle to the bathroom, filled it with water, and neatly returned it to the dresser.

That evening as we sat for dinner, Gramps hovered over me as he cut corn from the cob on my plate. He then commented, "Something smells good …kind of like flowers or something."

I put my head down and dug into my food (kind of like the Twix commercials when people stuff their mouth to avoid conversation). Grams looked at me suspiciously, and I'm guessing that when he made his comment, he added a wink (out of my sight) to Grams as he said it.

After we ate and cleaned up, Grams nonchalantly went to her room and came out to tell me it was bedtime and told Gramps, "Pete, thank you for my new bottle of perfume." I thought I was off the hook. But after she tucked me in and we said our prayers, she said in a firm voice, "Marissa, please do not play with my bottles. It is not safe for you."

I agreed and fell asleep holding Ricky Bear, who somehow had a trace of Evening in Paris on his fur.

Marissa Madrid

Journal:

Reflect on any positive events that occurred in your day. Pen it in your journal and list five different ways you can extend the experience each day.

Hands on Senses:

Many of us devote our last minutes before rest to stressful thoughts and worries. Make a valiant effort to redirect this toward imagining five ways you will extend your more joyful experiences.

Things to be grateful for upon resting:

- A bed or place you have to rest in
- Eyes to see life and to read enrichments of the mind
- Ears to hear birds, music, and words of meaning
- Lungs to breath the abundance of air
- The blood which runs through your veins and beating heart
- Sense of touch for feeling soft sheets and blankets

- Talents and skills, great and small

- The achievements you have already made

- Goals, determination and desire to reach your goals

- An imagination to create with

- A sense of humor to laugh in the face of fear

- Free will to make positive changes

- Resources waitng to be discovered for success

- To be born as a unique and unrepeated miracle

- The ability to make and build

- The option to be happy

- People who support and contribute to your vision

- The ability to believe in your worth

- The morning of a new day to make great things happen

- The opportunity to be a significant part of the world around you

Defining Yourself

Whenever I contemplated a decision in childhood and peer pressure was a factor, Grams's words were engraved in my mind: "Tell me who your friends are and I'll tell you who you are." It didn't always work, and I did find a few temptations, like eating more than my share of chocolate covered cherries a bit irresistible. But she was right. And now as an adult, a colleague of mine provided me with another version of that quote: "Take a look at your current circle of influence, and you can determine what your success will be ten years from now."

It's a given that we hit flat spots in our attitudes and perception of life. And we can submit to the black hole of feeling drained and motionless ... or we can take control. In my day-to-day business with individuals from diverse backgrounds, I hear people express why they cannot advance to a better life. The answer to that life is not printed on the green paper they so eagerly seek.

If your goal is money in hand without regard to other visions, then you're working for printed paper. If you love the tasks you perform as a part of you, the dream begins to unfold. As the dream unfolds, more dreams are created, and the momentum multiplies into aspirations of continual advancement.

Typical perceptions of advancement:

- "I'm getting another raise in four months."
- "I'm getting promoted next year."
- "Once I get a bonus, we can go camping."

Everything is based on waiting for another person to tell you your worth.

"Here, Bob. You're worth another sixty-five cents per hour. You can have your raise now. If you give up a little more time with your family, we can get you another ten cents on the umpteenth of Juvember."

It actually sounds confusing if you think about it. The point I'm making here is that you *can* think outside of the box. Believing in your vision and taking a class, hobby, or anything that enriches your soul will lead to greater things. People always say why they can't follow a vision. Switch it up and write down why you *can*. List all of your qualities and again validate that you *can* move forward.

Try it like this:

Vision = More time for health, wealth, and enjoyable activities.

Qualities = Alert, detail oriented, punctual, personable, conscientious, positive, healthy, motivated, intelligent, professional, courteous, teachable, responsible, skilled, helpful, compassionate.

These are all commonsense attributes as the foundation to seeking out your calling. You are so much more than a title!

Faith = Belief in self, working from the end, dictating what *you* want, listening to what makes you feel happy and accomplished, surrounding yourself with those who support your theories and ideas, ability to relinquish doubts about your qualities, knowing that all obstacles can be passed and learned from.

Vision + Qualities + Faith = Success, beginning with more visions, momentum, wisdom, spiritual connection, freedom, independence, health, wealth, time, relief, ability to contribute more, respect, exhilaration, passion for what you do, and most importantly … a contagious form of *love* spread to those who you inspire and empower.

> *Clarity of mind means clarity of passion,*
> *too; this is why a great and clear mind loves*
> *ardently and sees distinctly what it loves.*
>
> *—Blaise Pascal*

As I shared with Nate, "For every question you ask, the answer is always in the mirror."

Another key element to being deliberate and precise in defining what you truly want is to know yourself. Can you sit in complete silence thinking or noticing the details of your hands? We know that no two sets of fingerprints are the same. I'd like to think of this as another symbol that every individual is born with their own unique purpose and role to play in our great universe.

With your life as the canvas, everything is a masterpiece!

Conclusion

As a closing thought to all who read *Back When for Now:*

I sit here encountering not a conclusion, but a deep wish to enlighten just one person through these words. I want you to know that I was once a little girl and knew my calling; I was passionate in my mission to help others to believe in what the mind can conjure into existence, through the will of the one-and-only you: the beautiful, significant *you* who holds the definite power to create, love, and boldly stand in the face of all uncertainties as the leader of your life with the acceptance of humankind.

As we see what we imagine to be, I will always perceive living things as your thoughts, which created a realm connected to me. Go now, child, to that familiar place of forests, music, oceans, and colors; breathe, dance, and love; and share your well-intended passions with your sisters and brothers.

*Through the courage of one will, many paths are
laid forth and others follow in unity to aspire a
greater cause for humankind. M. Madrid*

Last, I briefly mentioned in the introduction that my Grandparents raised me. I will mention only but a few more thoughts about this experience, in honor of all Grandparents who have chosen this same act of faith and love.

By nature, you and your grandchildren will meet difficult times. By your patience and their innate eagerness to learn, there is a common ground where you share your world and life experiences with them; and they in turn reveal their's to you. Regardless of how your situation with them came to be, it is not yours, nor their fault. In this moment of confusion bound to repeat itself when they seek answers... most times the solution is in the distance between your arms and the warmth of your heart-with words of reassurance.

This relationship is like no other. It is not better. It is definitely not easier for either side. And, because there are more challenges, uncertainties, and unventured paths, some day those children as adults will reflect on a compelling history with you. It will be a story with double the love, strength, tenacity, and passion for a human life born with a purpose and function- exclusive to his or her fate of following you, as you lead by example. You may ask, "How is the story two fold?" To you I say, "The generation gap is not void and empty at all…but accommodates plenty more than what could be squeezed in the last time."

And, to the grandchildren, your Golden Parents are not mean, but wise. They are a living documentary of more than you can imagine or comprehend for now. Trust them. It was their free will and love for you to do what is right. Their other option was to do what's easy and walk away. In moments of doubt, loneliness, and sadness they will be the ones who feel your grief. Give them a chance. Know their priceless value to your life's journey. You will never know a greater love of its like.

Be well and be good to eachother on your preciously intended walk together.

Resources

Grandparents:

http://www.raisingyourgrandchildren.com/

http://www.usa.gov/Topics/Grandparents.shtml

http://www.grandparentsmagazine.net/rights.htm

Child Heroes of Inspiration: www.myhero.com/myhero/hero.asp?hero=childheroes

Marissa's Photography Gallery: www.yessy.com/4mymstudio (all photos included in back when for now were taken by Marissa Madrid and most are available for viewing at this site)

Collage Ideas: www.creativity-portal.com/howto/artscrafts/collage.html

Books and Supplies for Beading:

Chinese Knots for Beaded Jewelry by Suzen Millodot

Making Metal Jewelry: Projects, Techniques, Inspiration by Joanna Gollberg

The Encyclopedia of Jewelry-Making Techniques: A Comprehensive Visual Guide to Traditional and Contemporary Techniques by Jinks McGrath

www.jewelrysupply.com

www.asianartmall.com

www.specialtybeads.com

Vision Board Ideas: christinekane.com/blog/how-to-make-avision-board/

Creative Thank You Cards and More: www.paperwishes.com/products/7110

Inspirational E-cards: allgreen.smilestarters.com

Shadowbox Treasure Chest Ideas:

www.expertvillage.com/interviews/shadow-box.htm

www.monsterunderthebed.net/fun_stuff/How_to_Make_a_Treasure_Chest.pdf

A Little Book of Listening Skills: 52 Essential Practices for Profoundly Loving Yourself and Other People by Mark Brady and Jennifer Austin Leigh

Wisdom of Listening by Mark Brady

Healthier Thoughts

www.brainsync.com/a-z.asp

www.michaelgelb.com

www.blm.gov/education/lnt/tips.html

www.beyondtheveil.net/meditation.html

2007 Top 100 Children's Books: www.nea.org/readacross/resources/catalist.html

Tactile

www.silk.org.uk/history.htm

www.amtamassage.org/publications/massage.html

www.tooblessed2bestressed.com/

www.kaboose.com/craft-recipes.html

Scents and Taste

www.skepdic.com/aroma.html

www.sfherb.com/potpourri-ingredients.asp

www.spices101.com/index.html

Nutrition

www.ific.org

www.top100recipesites.com

www.drtoast.com/crumbs/108

www.mylifeinmynd.info

Activity

mercola.com/nutritionplan/exercise.htm

www.americanheart.org/presenter.jhtml?identifier=4563

Sleep

www.sleepfoundation.org

www.sleepeducation.com

www.brainsync.com/a-z.asp

www.neuroacoustic.com/sleep.html

personal-development.com/chuck/power-nap.htm

Environmental Wellness

environmentpsychology.com/green_design.htm

www.usace.army.mil/publications/design-guides/dg1110-3-122/c-2.pdf

www.highlysensitivesouls.com/

eartheasy.com/live_nontoxic_solutions.htm

www.newlifeinmynd.info

Inspiration and Attitude

www.simpletruths.com

www.tut.com

www.bradyates.net

www.facethecity.com

The Four Agreements by Don Miguel Ruiz

The Fifth Mountain by Paulo Coelho

The Millionaire's Course by Marc Allen

Discover Your Genius: How to Think Like History's Ten Most Revolutionary Minds by Michael Gelb

How to Think Like Leonardo da Vinci: Seven Steps to Genius Every Day by Michael J. Gelb

The Artist's Way by Julia Cameron

Jenna Avery, CLC, Life Coach for Sensitive Souls, has opened quite a few doors for me through her personal work and resources. This link provides alternative concepts for those who may struggle with overstimulation or question the direction they are headed toward. I recommend her site for much more than this, but you decide what works for you: www.highlysensitivesouls.com/articles/livingyourcalling.htm

About the Author

Marissa Madrid is a Colorado native. She has worked with children, families, and individuals for eighteen years as an educator, advocate, and community liaison. Marissa continues her vision to serve others in effort to strive for unified success in education, community development, and humanitarian goals to create a viable resources to all. She enjoys photography, rock hunting with her son, and observing life as it unfolds around her.